Fancy Goldfish

Paul Paradise

© T.F.H. Publications, Inc.

Distributed in the UNITED STATES to the Pet Trade by T.F.H. Publications, Inc., 1 TFH Plaza, Neptune City, NJ 07753; on the Internet at www.tfh.com; in CANADA by Rolf C. Hagen Inc., 3225 Sartelon St., Montreal, Quebec H4R 1E8; Pet Trade by H & L Pet Supplies Inc., 27 Kingston Crescent, Kitchener, Ontario N2B 2T6; in ENGLAND by T.F.H. Publications, PO Box 74, Havant PO9 5TT; in AUSTRALIA AND THE SOUTH PACIFIC by T.F.H. (Australia), Pty. Ltd., Box 149, Brookvale 2100 N.S.W., Australia; in NEW ZEALAND by Brooklands Aquarium Ltd., 5 McGiven Drive, New Plymouth, RD1 New Zealand; in SOUTH AFRICA by Rolf C. Hagen S.A. (PTY.) LTD., P.O. Box 201199, Durban North 4016, South Africa; in JAPAN by T.F.H. Publications. Published by T.F.H. Publications, Inc.
MANUFACTURED IN THE
UNITED STATES OF AMERICA
BY T.F.H. PUBLICATIONS, INC.

CONTENTS

HISTORY AND DESCRIPTION

Goldfish have been with us for over 1000 years. The typical goldfish as we know it today does not occur in the wild but is said to have been bred by the Chinese from natural mutations of the wild Crucian carp, a popular food fish. While goldfish were mentioned in Chinese poetry as early as 800 AD, it is believed that they did not arrive in Europe until about 1600; they were frequently mentioned by learned European authors of that era. The original wild variety of goldfish still exists in rivers and sluggish streams of its native China, where its somber olive color blends in with murky waters, providing the fish with excellent camouflage. Even today, the young of most domesticated goldfish varieties start life with the same somber coloring, only attaining the peak of their characteristic golden hue when they are about one year old.

Because of their beautiful coloring and often extreme hardiness, goldfish have become one of the most popular pets in the world. So popular are they that they are given away at carnivals and circuses in games of chance! Until recently, a spherical or drum-shaped bowl containing a couple of miserable-looking goldfish was a common feature in many homes. Unknown to their well-intentioned keepers, however, the very shape of the bowl provided an insufficient surface area for the absorption of oxygen and the

A class act! An A-Grade red and white hamanashiki with perfect body and different colors on each side of the body. A hamanashiki looks very much like a pearlscaled oranda except that the headgrowth is in two uniform bumps on the head. Photo by F. Rosenzweig.

3

dissipation of carbon dioxide, giving them poor water conditions and a very lethargic appearance. Fortunately, this fishbowl concept is almost a thing of the past in Western countries, and goldfish are now being displayed in rectangular tanks or, even more appropriately, in garden ponds.

EXTERNAL FEATURES

The goldfish, *Carassius auratus*, belongs to the carp family, which is known as Cyprinidae. Most carp possess barbels on their lips, but in the case of goldfish the barbels are absent. The dorsal fin of the goldfish is normally straight or slightly concave.

Over the centuries breeders have produced many weird and bizarre goldfish varieties, but it was the Japanese who, by selective breeding, produced a great many of the varieties. The fancy goldfish as we know it today can be shaped like a golf ball, have fins that exceed the length of its body, or eyes that look to the heavens. These features—and many more—are part and parcel of what makes a goldfish fancy.

Many people, when thinking of a pet fish, envision a common goldfish. The common goldfish possesses all of the typical fish characteristics: streamlined and scale-covered body, gill covers, large

lidless eyes, large mouth and, of course, fins. The fins of a fish have three main functions: stabilization, braking and, to some extent, propulsion. It is the caudal fin (tail) that seems to show the greatest variation between goldfish strains, often appearing as a single fin, a paired fin or any intermediate variation with pointed, squared, forked, rounded, short or long ends.

To obtain the necessary oxygen, fish draw water through the mouth, over the delicate gill filaments and finally pass it out through the opercula or gill covers. This process removes precious oxygen from the water via fine

A common goldfish. Photo by M. Gilroy.

An A-Grade red ryukin with a white face. This fish shows excellent matching of the fins to the body. Compared to the common goldfish, it is hard to believe that this fish shares the same lineage. Photo by F. Rosenzweig.

A celestial goldfish and a young comet. Photo by M. Gilroy.

This is a tank of "feeder" goldfish. Do not choose pet goldfish from a feeder tank. These fish do not receive the same care as pet fish and are unlikely to live long or well. Photo by D. Zoffer.

capillaries in the gill filaments and passes it into the fish's bloodstream, just as oxygen is removed via lung capillaries in higher vertebrates.

Simultaneously, carbon dioxide is expelled from the bloodstream and discharged into the water passing over the gills, thus the fish's respiratory wastes are removed from its body just as similar wastes are removed from our bodies via our lungs. When the water is polluted or deficient in oxygen (as it often is in a typical goldfish bowl), the goldfish congregate at the surface where the oxygen is being dissolved into the water. When goldfish hang from the surface with their gills making popping noises, they are actually gasping for oxygen in the air to avoid suffocation. This behavior indicates, of course, that the fish need immediate attention.

Unlike most higher animals, in which the nostrils open internally into the respiratory system, the nostrils of fishes are merely deadened pits that house scent buds. The scent buds are innervated and connect via the nervous system directly to the brain.

Fish possess no external ears, although they do have an internal ear. The internal ear serves the fish mostly as an organ of balance rather than hearing. To detect noises or vibrations in the water, most fishes have a lateral line. This consists of a row of pores that runs horizontally along the sides of the fish. The pores contain nerve cells, or neuromasts, and are interconnected by a canal that runs under the skin. The neuromasts in each pore are also interconnected and run

An A-Grade massive red cap headgrowth with a pure white body. This is a tremendous headgrowth. By the standards, the red cap oranda should have an all white body. The red headgrowth should be confined to the top of the head above the eye line. The fish can be fully hooded but the red coloration should be on top, like a cap. Photo by F. Rosenzweig.

directly to the brain via the same cranial nerve that connects to the ears in higher animals.

The eyes of goldfish are fairly large, lidless and somewhat moveable. Goldfish are generally believed to be nearsighted, but their eyesight seems to be adequate for their needs. Highly developed goldfish strains with telescope and bubble eyes have a more restricted field of vision than do goldfish with normal eyes, but when they are well cared for in an aquarium they seem to have no difficulty finding their way around.

The body of the goldfish is covered with overlapping scales, which are hard plates set beneath a thin layer of epidermal tissue. The scales offer the fish protection against injury and infection. There are also numerous mucous glands in the skin that produce the characteristic slimy surface on the fish. This slime coating also protects the fish against injury and disease. In addition, the slime reduces friction between the fish and its watery environment, making it easier for the fish to swim.

The size of the scales varies with the size and age of the fish. Good scale shape and definition are important in creating the correct body outline. All goldfish have scales, but some strains are erroneously known as "scaleless." On these fish the scales are less conspicuous because they lack the layer of pigment, sometimes known as guanine, that normally renders them opaque and gives them their metallic iridescence. The amount of this pigment apparent in a fish is at least partly governed by inheritance but is also governed by envi-

7

A fantail goldfish undergoing a color change. Photo by M. Gilroy.

ronmental factors such as the fish's food. Goldfish that do not have much of this reflective pigment in their scales are termed "matt" fish, while fish having a good supply of guanine under all of their scales are termed "metallic." Goldfish with a combination of metallic and matt scales are called "nacreous." Genetically speaking, neither metallic nor matt scales are completely dominant. Nacreous appears to be an intermediate state of scale coloration that is produced by crossing a metallic fish to a matt fish. Goldfish whose scales are entirely of the matt type are seldom seen commercially because they do not show the intense coloration of the metallic fish, nor are they as hardy.

This is a black lionhead slowly changing into a red and black. The headgrowth is weak, and the fish has only a slight slope to the body and tail. Photo by F. Rosenzweig.

Each variety of goldfish has a specific number of scales that remains constant, barring accidental loss. As the fish grows, each scale grows at its periphery. During the winter when the water is cooler, growth slows down or stops altogether, depending upon how cool the fish is kept. When the pond water warms up in the spring and the fish once more begins to feed heavily, rapid growth starts again. This slowing down and reacceleration of the growth process causes rings to form on the scales, and the number of rings on each scale indicates the age of the fish—one ring represents one year's growth.

At 60 days of age, most goldfish that hatch having the protective Crucian coloration usually begin to lose their color. The scales blacken and then begin to fade, starting at the belly area and progressing upward toward the back. When these fish have completed the phase they are usually yellow in color, but with the passage of time their color intensifies, once more giving them a darker appearance. Not all goldfish strains undergo this decoloration. Some may never decolor while others may not do so until they are several years old. Matt fish never pass through this color change because they hatch light in color (often white) and gradually darken as their colors intensify. The ultimate color of a goldfish is strongly influenced by its diet and the chemical composition of the water in which it is reared as well as by its genetic endowments.

There is a wide range of foods available for goldfish in both flake and pellet forms and in different sizes and formulations—hobbyists can even choose between sinking and floating pellets. Photo courtesy of Wardley Corporation.

This red and white metallic ranchu shows the typical curved back and sports beautifully sequined scales with random brocaded scales. Photo by F. Rosenzweig.

This matt ranchu is 5 years old, weighs two pounds, and is 10 inches in length! Photo by F. Rosenzweig.

GOLDFISH VARIETIES

There are many different varieties of goldfish, and most of them are derived from the same original stock by the careful breeding of selected fish. Most of the varieties were originally developed in China or Japan. The original strains probably came from China, but the Japanese can take credit for developing the more beautiful varieties.

COMMON GOLDFISH

All goldfish, regardless of their variety, have the same scientific name, *Carassius auratus*, but the only one that resembles its original ances-tors very much is the common goldfish. This variety has a slender body and, when very young, its black pigmentation gives it the appearance of dull steel blue. The color gradually changes as the fish gets older to a vermilion red, often with white patches. The tail is forked.

The common goldfish is very hardy. This is an ideal pond fish that can withstand even extreme temperatures as long as they are brought about gradually. They will eat just about anything. They are prolific and enthusiastic breeders.

COMET

The comet goldfish is an American breed that is slim and lean and will grace any pond or aquarium. The single tail fin is as long or longer than the body in high quality fish and each lobe comes to a point. All the other fins of the comet are much longer than the normal singletailed breeds.

WAKIN

The wakin is a Japanese fish that is very similar to the common goldfish. It has short fins and a stocky body with a double caudal fin. This is a very active fish that should not be kept with slow or delicate goldfish.

JIKIN

The jikin, or peacock tail, was developed from the wakin and possesses a typical gold-fish shape. All the fins are short and the tail is X-shaped when viewed from the rear.

SHUBUNKIN

There are two types of this singletailed breed. One has a long tail fin with broad tail fin lobes that are rounded on the end. The other has a short tail fin like the common goldfish. What makes these fish a particular breed is that they are of the nacreous scale group (calico) which are primarily bred for their beautiful colors. Red, black, and sky blue are the perfect colors of the calico breeds and the shubunkin come closer than any other breed to these ideals. The long bodies are typically fish shaped, like the common goldfish.

This is the best way to view jikins—in a group. Jikins are elongated, delicate goldfish with pearl white bodies and red on all the fins. The caudals are widely spread and the double tail fin has a pronounced X shape. Other names include peacock tail. Photo by F. Rosenzweig.

This is nice conformation in a red oranda with a longer body form adapted to swimming in the greater space of a natural pond. Photo by F. Rosenzweig.

FANTAIL

The fantail is the common commercial doubletailed breed of the retail market. Its body is longer than the oranda but shorter than the singletail breeds. The head of the fantail comes to a point and it has no head growth. The tail finnage should be long and flowing. More fantails are sold every year than any other doubletailed breed. They are tough and do equally well in a pond or aquarium. This should be the first doubletailed breed of the beginner as they are easy to care for.

This fish is a telescope-eyed veiltail. Photo by F. Rosenzweig.

This is a shubunkin, ideal for both aquaria and ponds. Photo by F. Rosenzweig.

GOLDFISH VARIETIES

Foods formulated specifically for goldfish take into account the fact that goldfish need foods containing less protein and fat and more plant fiber than other diets provide. Photo courtesy of O.S.I. Marine Lab., Inc.

This is a rare matt shubunkin. The matt scaling on this fish makes it appear almost scaleless. Photo by F. Rosenzweig.

VEILTAILS

Veiltails are often confused with fantails; however, the veiltail has a divided caudal fin that is so long and full that it hangs down in graceful folds. Veiltails also have a high, elegant dorsal fin. The head is pointed. The double tail fins of the veiltail have no indentation between the lobes. This square cut tail and the very high erect dorsal fin are the features that characterize this breed. The veiltail finnage can be, and has been, bred into many breeds of goldfish. Orandas, telescopes, moors, and pearlscales have all had veiltails bred into them. Pure veiltails are not easy to find and are considered to be very rare in the United States.

This is the form one wants to see in a red veiltail. Notice that not only are the caudal and dorsal fins extra long but that the pectorals and ventrals are exaggerated also. Photo by F. Rosenzweig.

This is a striking red veiltail with squared fins a full 150 percent the size of the body. The excellent dorsal is almost as high as the good egg-shaped body is deep. Photo by F. Rosenzweig.

This is a pompon veiltail raised in an outdoor pond showing the slender body of an outdoor fish. The pompons are well developed. Photo by F. Rosenzweig.

This fish is a massive 10-inch veiltail with a large egg-shaped body and a small face. Veiltails have caudal finnage that has little or no forking or indentation between the top and bottom tail fin lobes. The dorsal should be high, 50-100 percent of the depth of the body. Ideally it should be held erect but as fish get older and larger that is rarely the case. The body should be round, deep, and egg-shaped. The caudal fin should be one to two times the body length. Photo by F. Rosenzweig.

ORANDA

This doubletailed breed is one of the most popular and beautiful of all the goldfish. The oranda has a head growth, which, in most breeds, covers the whole head. The goosehead and the redcap oranda mainly have the growth limited to the top of the head, which forms a high cap. The body of the oranda is short and round with flowing fins.

Right: A new and possibly unstable color combination known as lilac oranda. The off-brown coloration appears lilac in sunlight. The fish shown is a lilac oranda with massive headgrowth that even covers the eyes. The fish is weighed down due to the headgrowth and swims poorly. This is not a candidate for the garden pond. Photo by F. Rosenzweig.

This is the Japanese-style calico oranda known as the azumanishiki with a longer body, metallic scales, and less thickness to headgrowth and longer finnage than the Western-style orandas. Photo by F. Rosenzweig.

Red faced and red capped orandas. A red-faced oranda differs from a red cap in that the red extends all over the face. Photo by F. Rosenzweig.

A fleshlike tissue known as headgrowth surrounding all or parts of the facial area characterizes Orandas. There are many variations of headgrowth, finnage, body shape, and color. This is a rare broadtail oranda, an oranda with veiltail characteristics of veil-like square caudal fins and a high, square dorsal that is almost as deep as the body. Photo by F. Rosenzweig.

This is an older 2-pound full hooded red oranda. The headgrowth has been cut away from the eyes and manicured to allow the fish some vision. Photo by F. Rosenzweig.

An A-Grade black calico oranda with perfect conformation and balance of fins to body. The headgrowth shows beautiful coloring with gray markings. Photo by F. Rosenzweig.

Here is a beautiful orange oranda with black trim on the fins and a black moustache. Photo by F. Rosenzweig.

RANCHU

This dorsalless breed was developed in Japan. This short, round-bodied fish has a broad head covered with a generous head growth. All of the fins are short with the double tail fin being attached to the caudal peduncle at a sharp angle. The tail fin is held erect and can be fully divided or partially webbed. The curvature along the back is a smooth arch with a sharp angle downward as it nears the caudal peduncle.

Right: This is an incredible 2 1/2-pound ranchu. Photo by F. Rosenzweig.

This is a 2-year-old ranchu with a beautiful form, solid red with symmetrical fins, and a deep, round body. Photo by F. Rosenzweig.

A group of excellent ranchus. Photo by F. Rosenzweig

Jet black coloring in a black ranchu with a high back and deep tailset. Photo by F. Rosenzweig.

This is a ranchu-lionhead combination with the thicker and broader head like a lionhead. Photo by F. Rosenzweig.

An A-Grade red and white lionhead with a beautiful solid red headgrowth extending well beyond the body. This fish has exceptional headgrowth and a beautiful smooth back. Photo by F. Rosenzweig.

This is a 12-inch red and white lionhead with excellent headgrowth and back contour. Photo by F. Rosenzweig.

An A-Grade fish. This red and white lionhead displays a fantastic hood. Note the massive thickness of the headgrowth and yet the fish still swims properly. Photo by F. Rosenzweig.

LIONHEAD

This is another dorsalless breed that has the same general characteristics as the ranchu. This Chinese breed is much sought after and probably has the largest head growth of all varieties. A double tail propels the short boxy body. View this tail from above and the tail looks like butterfly wings. The back outline is straighter than found in the ranchu, but it still has a gentle, even curve, which is carried right to the caudal peduncle.

Right: This is a beautiful rare white-faced lionhead with excellent facial features. Photo by F. Rosenzweig.

Above: Lionheads with blunt, square faces. Photo by F. Rosenzweig.

Left: An A-Grade red cap lionhead. Photo by F. Rosenzweig.

BUBBLE-EYE

The outstanding feature of the bubble-eye as the name indicates is a pair of large fluid-filled bubbles under each eye that wobble as the fish swims. The bubble-eye has no dorsal fin and should have no head growth. The bubbles (from bubble to bubble) can be as wide as the fish is long, which is astounding in a large adult bubble-eye. The body is long and torpedo-shaped with long flowing double tail fins.

This red and white bubble-eye shows good eye attachment below the eye affording better vision than usual. Photo by F. Rosenzweig.

A trio of calico bubble-eyes. Photo by F. Rosenzweig.

This calico bubble-eye shows a perfectly smooth back, symmetrical eyes, a nice tail and good balance. Photo by F. Rosenzweig.

A calico bubble-eye with beautiful marking on one side. Photo by F. Rosenzweig.

The result of a bubble-eye/oranda cross.

TELESCOPE

This breed has eyes that protrude from the head (globe-eye). The eyes are much larger than are found in normal-eyed fish, and the shape can vary from fish to fish. In selecting this doubletailed breed, pay special attention to both eyes, making sure they are the same size and shape. The body of this breed is short and round. This is one of the few breeds where a solid black color over the entire body can be found. The black telescope is called a Moor.

Telescope eyes are the most varied of all the goldfish breeds with regard to finnage, body form, color, etc. One thing they have in common is that they all have telescope eyes, eyes that are mounted on conelike stalks and extend outward. Eyes may vary in size from fish to fish but should be the same size on a single specimen. The eyes are fragile and care must be taken to treat them gently. Photo by F. Rosenzweig.

Below: This is a rare and unusual black pearlscale hamanashiki with telescope eyes. Photo by F. Rosenzweig.

Below: This is a very rare chocolate butterfly telescope eye. It is a large fish with good square caudals. (Little indentation between the top and bottom tailfin lobes.) If the squared caudals were longer and the dorsal higher, this would be a broadtail variety. Photo by F. Rosenzweig.

A red telescope eye with white face and two puffy red pompons. Telescope eyed pompons are elongated fish with telescope eyes and expanded nasal passages resembling pompons. Photo by F. Rosenzweig.

A champion 2-pound calico telescope butterfly, a massive 6-year-old fish. Photo by F. Rosenzweig.

CELESTIAL

This unique dorsalless breed has a long torpedo-shaped body with long fins. The eyes of the celestial protrude from the head like they do in telescopes, but in the celestial, the eyes turn to gaze upward at a very early age. The eyes are encased in a hard covering and should be the same size and look in the same direction. The pupils should be the same size also.

Right: Celestial goldfish. Photo by M. Gilroy.

Chocolate pompon celestials, new color development in celestial with pompon nasal passages. Photo by F. Rosenzweig.

POMPON

Another dorsalless breed but this one has a short, round boxy body like a lionhead with a short double tail fin. The nasal septa (narial flaps) have been enlarged and folded so many times that they take on the appearance of velvety peas. Older pompons will develop a small head growth. Pompon orandas, lionheads, and hanafusa (dorsaled pompons) are available from time to time. In some of these breeds the pompons are not much more than ruffled nose flaps almost covered by head growth ranging to long, flowing, ruffled streamers with no head growth.

Some pompons have difficulty breathing because the pompons obstruct their mouths.

Pompon red and white goldfish. Photo by M. Gilroy

Gold celestial pompon out of water with a view of encased eyes and pompons. Photo by F. Rosenzweig.

A red telescope eye with many pompons fused together. Photo by F. Rosenzweig

RYUKIN

The ryukin is a very round-bodied goldfish that in the highly developed humpbacked variety looks like a ball with fins and head attached to it. The ryukin is one of the most popular goldfish breeds and is a very good breed for beginners to start with. Ryukins are brightly colored and can be found in red, red and white, white, and the best calicos of any of the double tailfinned breeds.

Right: This is a rare blue-scaled ryukin with wonderful finnage and shoulder hump. Photo by F. Rosenzweig.

Right: An incredibly marked "tiger striped" ryukin. Photo by F. Rosenzweig.

Left: This is a rare brown ryukin with rich coloring and a nice shoulder hump. Photo by F. Rosenzweig.

A beautifully finned scarlet red and white ryukin. Photo by F. Rosenzweig.

A black and gold pearlscale with a massive body, small face, and beautiful lateral line with the pearl scales running up the back and along the lateral line. Photo by F. Rosenzweig.

PEARLSCALE

This very round-bodied breed has a scale type all its own. In high quality fish each scale has a hard raised area in the center of each scale. This raised area is usually white in color and looks like a half pearl pasted to each scale, thus the name pearlscale. The double tail fin is square cut like the veiltail. In the last few years, pearlscales have been seen with oranda headgrowth, long fins, and longer bodies. It seems there are a lot of people doing a lot of work with this breed.

A pair of rare chocolate hamanashikis. Hamanashiki is essentially a pearlscaled oranda. Photo by F. Rosenzweig.

This is a very rare calico broadtail pearlscale with typical scaling but with long caudal finnage with little forking and a high, square dorsal. Photo by F. Rosenzweig.

Three distinctly different headgrowths on hamanashiki. Photo by F. Rosenzweig.

Avoid keeping fast, slim goldfish with slower fancy varieties. The slower fish will not be able to compete for food and will lose thrift. Photo by M.P. & C. Piednoir.

SELECTING YOUR GOLDFISH

The young of most goldfish strains bear little resemblance to their parents. It usually takes from one to two years for young goldfish to develop their special characteristics. For this reason, mature fancy goldfish are quite costly, while young specimens are far less expensive. The best time of the year to buy young goldfish is in September or October, purchasing fish of the spring hatching. By this time, the bodies of the young fish should be about 1.5 inches long. Two inches or more is even better.

Select healthy, active fish from a tank of healthy fish. If there are any sick fish in the tank, it's a good bet all may become sick. Never buy fish that float at the surface whenever they stop swimming. Make sure the fish you choose have a full complement of intact fins and body parts. While a damaged fin will regrow, an eye won't. Damaged fins will continue to deteriorate, however, if the cause of the damage is not corrected. If you have your heart set on a fish with some damage, be sure you know how to treat the problem or else select an undamaged fish.

There are hundreds of varieties of goldfish. Pick what you find attractive. It is best not to mix wild-type goldfish and slower, heavy bodied fancy goldfish. The sleeker wild-type will get all the food in a mixed group.

Left: This is a rare blue-scaled, violet-hued telescope eye with chocolate finnage. A rare and costly specimen such as this should not be put in a tank with any fish that would harass it. Photo by F. Rosenzweig.

GOLDFISH CARE

Your goldfish aquarium should be purchased, set up, and the water aged and conditioned before you buy the fish. In order to purchase the right aquarium, you should have some idea of the kind and number of goldfish you want to buy. First, let's look at the procedure for selecting the right equipment and setting it up.

THE AQUARIUM

If you intend to become a serious goldfish keeper, you should consider purchasing a standard rectangular aquarium rather than the traditional goldfish bowl. To properly keep a one-inch goldfish you should have *at least* a one-gallon aquarium with a water surface area of about 70 to 90 square inches. This automatically excludes most bowls. While a one-gallon bowl may hold the right amount of water for a small goldfish, most bowls are round and narrower at the top than they are in the middle. If a one-gallon bowl is filled with water, the water surface near the top is much less than it is at the middle of the bowl; however, if you fill the bowl only to the middle, it will not have enough water in it for the goldfish to survive.

In China, very exotic goldfish are kept in large ceramic containers outdoors. While these containers have no filtration or aeration, they are *not* the same as the standard goldfish bowl. They hold a goodly amount of water and are wide at the top for good

High quality, very expensive rich black ranchus with good headgrowth, excellent body, and super color! The only way to raise fish like this is to give them the very best of everything...water quality, room to grow, and good food. Photo by F. Rosenzweig.

This deep-bodied, 2-year-old female ranchu is showing rich, deep color and high-contrast white. Often, this quality of fish is raised in protected sunlit pools. Photo by F. Rosenzweig.

gas exchange. Most importantly, the goldfish are well cared for and given a lot of attention so if anything were to go wrong, it would be quickly discovered and corrected.

A rectangular aquarium has the same surface area at the center as it does at the top. Maximum air-water interface is important because most of the oxygen in the water is absorbed at the surface. By restricting this surface, as you would in a bowl, there will not be enough oxygen in the water for the fish to breathe properly. This large surface is also important to the goldfish because it allows a greater amount of carbon dioxide to be dispelled from the water than a small surface area would allow. In addition to lack of oxygen, excess carbon dioxide will cause the fish to suffocate.

While a one-inch goldfish can be kept in a one-gallon aquarium, that does not necessarily mean that a ten-inch goldfish can be kept in a ten-gallon aquarium. The amount of oxygen a fish consumes is determined by the fish's mass or weight, not by its length. A ten-inch goldfish weighs much more than ten times the weight of a one-inch goldfish, because in addition to being much longer, it is also much larger in girth. If your goldfish are properly cared for and well fed, they are going to grow quickly. With a few months of good care a one-inch goldfish can grow to a length of several inches, so a ten-gallon aquarium will not comfortably house ten one-inch goldfish either.

A ten-gallon aquarium is 20 inches long and 10 inches wide, so it has a surface area

of about 200 square inches. This means that it can comfortably house three or four small goldfish and will allow plenty of room for them to swim and grow—up to a point. Consider that your goldfish *will* grow. A five-gallon aquarium can comfortably hold a pair of small goldfish, and a 20-gallon tank (the 30-inch long style) can comfortably house six to eight fish. These aquaria can be more crowded than this, but that means more cleaning, more water changing and stronger filtration will be required.

THE BOTTOM LAYER

A two- to four-inch layer of sand or gravel should be placed on the bottom of the aquarium. The gravel will anchor the aquarium plants and will provide a more natural-looking environment for your goldfish. The sand or gravel should be fairly fine in texture (a 1/8-inch particle size is just about right). Coarser gravel will allow uneaten food particles to become trapped in the gravel bed, where they will decay, fouling the water and causing it to become cloudy with harmful, smelly bacteria.

The gravel should be washed before placing it in the tank. This is easily accomplished by putting it in a clean pan (making sure there is no soap or detergent residue in the pan) and running a gentle flow of tap water through the gravel, stirring and sifting until the water runs off clean and clear.

Colored gravels can be used in the goldfish aquarium. Just make sure that the gravel purchased is colorfast and

Rectangular aquaria are ideal for keeping goldfish. Make sure your tank is level before you fill it with water. Once the tank is filled, it will be very obvious if it is not level as the water line will be crooked relative to the tank frame. This will annoy you. Photo by F. Rosenzweig.

will not lose its dye in the water. While tinted water usually will not harm the fish, it certainly does not make them look very attractive. Most colored gravels manufactured specifically for aquarium use are colorfast. The use of dark gravel such as black, dark green, or dark blue gives the goldfish their best appearance. Lighter gravel will give the fish a washed-out look.

Be absolutely sure that the gravel you choose is smooth so it doesn't damage the mouths of these bottom-sifting goldfish. Avoid sharp and rough objects of any type in the aquarium.

Don't forget, you are perfectly free to use no gravel or substrate in the aquarium. This is the method preferred by professionals, a bare-bottom tank from which uneaten food and wastes can be efficiently siphoned for maximum water quality. You can reduce reflection from the bottom glass by painting the outside bottom of the tank a dark color with marine paint.

PLANTS IN THE AQUARIUM

Goldfish can be maintained quite successfully without live plants in the aquarium, but healthy plants help improve the water quality. Goldfish will nibble on soft-leaved plants; this greenery is an important part of the goldfish diet. Because of this, you don't really want to include expensive or rare plants in the goldfish aquarium. The best plants to begin with are *Elodea* (or anacharis, as it is often called) and *Cabomba*. Both are inexpensive, grow rapidly just floating in the water and don't require

Colorfast gravel can be used to accent the color of a particular fish. In this case, the use of blue gravel with a blue-scale oranda is a nice touch. Photo by M. Gilroy.

special care other than sufficient light, either from a sunlit window or from an aquarium light fixture. Once the aquarium is well established and the fish and plants are flourishing (usually this happens after a few months of good care), you can put some strongly rooted plants in the tank such as *Vallisneria*, *Sagittaria*, *Ludwigia* or Amazon sword plants. Java fern is practically indestructible, inedible, and looks fabulous when it attaches to a piece of rock or driftwood. Java fern does not require strong light either, which makes it a hit with people who do not want a brightly lit aquarium.

Goldfish look wonderful against a well-planted background. With a little care in your selection of plant species, you can keep your goldfish in a well-planted tank. Photo by M.P. & C. Piednoir.

THE WATER

Goldfish, even very fancy strains, are coldwater fish, so they don't require heated aquarium water. A water temperature of 68° F is considered ideal. Above 80° F some fish may suffer and even die. Below 50 degrees the fish will become lethargic and should not be fed. Room temperature water suits them well. But, like any other animal, they are liable to become ill if they are exposed to sudden drastic temperature changes, especially if the temperature is suddenly dropped. When their water needs to be changed, make sure the fresh water is of the same temperature as that in the tank. The best way to do this is to keep a clean plastic bucket of water aging for water changes. This way the water in both the tank and the bucket will both be at room temperature.

In addition to equalizing the temperature, storing the water allows time for the chlorine in it to dissipate into the air. The amount of chlorine in most tap water will kill goldfish, so it must somehow be removed from the water before the water can be used. Aging the water for at least 24 hours allows this to happen naturally. It's a good idea to keep a bottle of chemical chlorine remover handy in case your goldfish need a water change quickly when there is no aged water available.

In some areas, the municipal water is treated with chloramine. Aging the water does not remove chloramine. If your water contains chloramine, you must use a water conditioner that removes chlorine and chloramine. Chlorine and chloramine remover is available at your local pet shop.

In general, goldfish can adapt to almost any tap water hardness or pH, as long as changes are made slowly, over a few days. There is a natural tendency for the pH of aquarium water to drop over time and become more acidic. Your routine water changes will prevent this acidification from becoming a problem for your fish. Your life will be easier if you gradually acclimate your fish to your normal water conditions.

As a part of routine maintenance, one-fourth to one-third of the aquarium water should be changed weekly. For a small partial change like this, fresh tap water can be used without worrying about the chlorine in it harming your goldfish. The fresh water will be greatly diluted by the water remaining in your aquarium, so the chlorine will not be concentrated enough to harm the fish. The temperature must still be equalized before adding the new water to the tank.

AERATION

The function of an aerator is to agitate the water, which exposes a greater amount of water surface to the atmosphere. This facilitates the absorption of oxygen from the air and the dissipation of carbon dioxide and other gaseous wastes from the

When you fill that tank for the first time, give it some time to settle and for the gases to disperse before adding your fish. Photo by I. Francais.

water. An aerator is simply an apparatus that introduces a regular supply of air into the water via a stream of bubbles. That apparatus can be a small piston pump or a diaphragm vibrator, which is simply called a vibrator pump. Both are available in various price ranges, but the piston pump, which is much more powerful than the vibrator pump, is much more expensive, too. A piston pump will produce enough air to operate a number of aquaria at one time. But for the beginner or the fancier with only a few tanks, a vibrator pump is usually more than adequate. There are some good vibrator pumps available that are relatively inexpensive.

The air pump pushes air into the tank through the airline to which an airstone has been attached. Airstones are manufactured from a porous material through which the air is forced and emerges in the water as continuous streams of tiny bubbles.

FILTRATION

Unless you plan on performing massive daily water changes, a filter is a very necessary piece of aquarium equipment. Virtually all filters will clear the water by trapping particles of dirt, but they perform a more important function biologically. A new tank will experience "new tank syndrome," a condition of elevated ammonia and nitrite, when the fish are first introduced. This is very dangerous for your fish, as both ammonia and nitrite are very toxic to them. After a filter has been operating in the tank for a while (up to six

A box filter filled with floss and carbon is a very effective filter that has stood by the hobby for generations. Photo by I. Francias.

An air pump is versatile and very useful. It will provide the air you need to run your airlift-type filters and airstones. Photo by I. Francais.

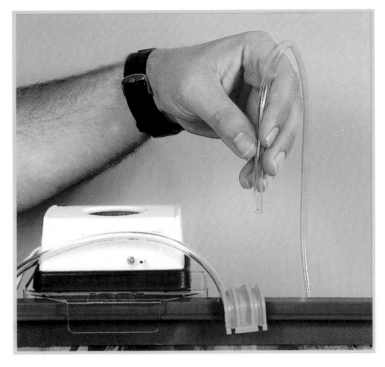

This tank is deep but because of its shape provides good surface area. Just to be on the safe side, use airstones and filters that provide good water movement to insure against low oxygen content in the water. Photo by I. Francais.

Canister filters are very important in the hobby, especially where delicate organisms are involved that need high quality water. Photo by Dr. H. R. Axelrod.

weeks for a brand-new tank) it becomes colonized by nitrifying bacteria. These bacteria are service-oriented and reduce the ammonia and nitrite. It is to the benefit of all concerned that these bacteria be treated with respect and lovingly cultivated. When you are cleaning your filter, retain some of the "dirt." This material is full of the nitrifying bacteria that will be continually replenished in the presence of ammonia and nitrite. When you are rinsing your filter media, use some tank water that you have siphoned out for this purpose. Hot or cold water will kill the bacteria.

When you start a new tank, there are some things you can do to get a head start on your nitrifying bacteria. The most common method is to use some gravel or filter material from a healthy tank. Alternatively, there are instant bacterial starter cultures available on the market that will seed your filter right away. Either method works just fine, and I highly recommend that you follow one of these methods. Failure to seed the filter will result in your fish being damaged as the ammonia and nitrite peak during the cycling of the tank.

Box Filter

There are many types of filters available, but the least expensive and, in many cases, the most practical for a small aquarium is the box filter. This simple filter consists of a plastic box with a platform for holding the filtering material. An airstone for lifting the water from underneath the platform is attached to an airline and pump. The inside of the box is filled with filter

This is an A-Grade hamanashiki. Fish of this quality cannot be produced in goldfish bowls. Goldfish hobbyists are enthusiastic and dedicated, and their fish show it! Photo by F. Rosenzweig.

A hood is an important piece of aquarium equipment. Even if you choose not to light the tank, the amount of water lost to evaporation on an open-top tank is considerable. One problem with evaporation is that the pollutants in the tank are concentrated as the water decreases. Photo by I. Francais.

Today's power filters are highly functional and often have excellent accessories such as micron or diatom filter components. Photo by I. Francais.

floss and perhaps activated carbon. By removing the water, a downward current is created to draw the aquarium water through the filtering material in the box. The filtering material usually consists of filter floss, which is intended to collect the large particles of debris in the water. Underneath the filter floss is very likely activated carbon. The efficiency of the carbon can vary, but a high grade of carbon will remove not only organic matter but also some metals and gases. In fact, when a tank is medicated the carbon is removed, as it will filter out medications, too. (The activated carbon part of the filter would then be providing chemical filtration.)

The box filter is versatile and inexpensive, and it can be moved from tank to tank. For example, it can be used in a new tank to avoid new tank syndrome because it will filter out organics and, at the same time, help seed the new tank with a colony of nitrifying bacteria. (Of course, this last part will work only if the filter has been used previously in an established aquarium.) It is advisable to change the filter material regularly, as the organic matter trapped in the carbon is still in contact with the water. Also, activated carbon loses its effectiveness in a relatively short time, so it needs to be replenished fairly frequently.

Sponge Filter

Sponge filters are both biological and mechanical filters that are used with an airline and air pump. Sponge filters should be squeezed out frequently to keep the pores from clogging and keep the

New and expensive, the tricolor—red, black, and white—ryukin will show up very well, especially in clean, clear water with good lighting. Photo by F. Rosenzweig.

filters at peak efficiency. They are inexpensive and handy, much like box filters, and they, too, can be moved around from tank to tank.

Power Filter

Power filters are motor-powered boxes that hang on the back or side of the tank. The water is drawn from the tank through a tube or hose into the media-filled box. Then the cleansed water overflows back into the tank.

It is important to clean the siphon tubes with a brush on a regular basis. Even the giant siphon tubes that are used tend to become coated with algae, and tests have shown that such growths greatly impede the flow of water through them.

Power filters are available in many sizes to service the smallest and the largest aquaria. There are many choices of media from pre-formed filter pads impregnated with carbon to sponge to special chemical media that remove specific toxins.

This may be the most important thing you do for your goldfish...regular partial water changes. The frequent application of fresh water is the best tonic, growth and appetite stimulant, and disease preventative known in fishkeeping. Photo by I. Francais.

Canister Filter

The canister filter is the workhorse of the aquarium. The advantage to this device is that it pumps the water under pressure. That way the water can be processed much faster than by even an outside power filter. Technically, of course, the canister filter *is* an outside filter and is powered, too. It is simply the evolution of that type of filter into its most advantageous form. The water is removed rapidly out of the tank and run through the filter media, then returned to the tank. Often it is returned via a spray bar, which provides the aeration that might otherwise have been missing. Besides, the rapid turnover of water keeps the

This is a massive 5-year-old ranchu with the highly developed headgrowth that comes only with age. Photo by F. Rosenzweig.

water in the tank circulating so that there is a more efficient gas exchange at the surface, for all of the water is eventually circulated there, and it happens more quickly with a canister filter. A further advantage of the canister filter is that, since the water is under pressure, it will not go around the filter media as it begins to clog up with material. For the goldfish tank, however, it is necessary to use a prefilter on a canister filter. Canister filters should not need frequent cleaning, and a prefilter will go a long way to keeping the canister clean and performing as the biological filter it is meant to be. Without a prefilter, too much solid waste enters the canister and it will have to be disturbed much more frequently, not a desirable situation.

LIGHTING

Goldfish don't particularly need artificial lighting to thrive, but plants do, and the fish do look best when kept in a lit aquarium. Fluorescent lights are the norm for aquaria these days and the best choice. Use a full hood and reflector. The use of a hood will reduce evaporation of the water and helps protect the fish from airborne pollutants.

AQUARIUM MAINTENANCE

Water changes are vital to the health and well being of your goldfish. Even with a good filtration system, harmful gases and substances will build up in the water. Ammonia, nitrites, and nitrates are all very harmful to goldfish and the best way to keep these

A butterfly tail. The two separate lobes look like butterfly wings when viewed from above. These fins are perfect, something not possible if the fish is kept in water polluted with bacteria, ammonia, nitrite, etc. To keep these delicate fins intact and in good condition, the water must be pristine. Photo by F. Rosenzweig.

A-Grade tremendous (9 inches) matt/metallic red and white ryukin with random sequined scales. Photo by F. Rosenzweig.

AA-Grade, 5-year-old champion red and white short-tail ryukin with a perfect shoulder hump. This fish weighs in at 2 1/2 pounds. Photo by F. Rosenzweig.

This is a virtually perfectly shaped edonoshiki calico ranchu. The back forms a smooth curve and arch with a perfect strong caudal and beautiful tail set. Excellent headgrowth with rich coloration. Photo by F. Rosenzweig.

waste, so these water changes are very important.

As the tank matures, algae will begin to appear on the glass and other tank surfaces. Algae are low forms of plant life, the spores of which can travel freely in both water and air. Eventually algae spores will find their way into almost any aquarium. The bright green algae provide some fresh food for the fish, to a limited degree help oxygenate the water and help absorb some of the byproducts of fish wastes as their food. The main problem with algae is that they grow all over the inner glass surfaces of the aquarium and make it difficult to see the fish. For a clear view of the fish, algae should be removed from the front glass and perhaps from the sides, too. This can be done with an inexpensive algae scraper purchased from a pet shop. Because of the benefit to the aquarium and the fish, it's a good idea to leave some of the algae in the tank, for instance on the back glass and on any rocks you have in the tank. In addition to these benefits, a small amount of algae also helps give the tank a more natural appearance.

harmful chemicals at low levels is to regularly change part of the water.

Depending on the tank or pond's population, temperature, filtration system, etc., a 10% to 50% partial water change is recommended every week. Goldfish are heavy feeders and produce a lot of

These young lionheads show nice blunt faces, nicely developing headgrowth, and smooth backs. Photo by F. Rosenzweig.

Live plants should be inspected often, and any dead or dying leaves or shoots should be removed. They can be easily removed by pinching them off between the thumb and forefinger.

Perfect A-Grade bluescale with violet hues showing up at the shoulder hump. This is a massive 8-inch female. Photo by F. Rosenzweig

From time to time it may be necessary to prune those plants that have grown too large. Cuttings from plants such as *Cabomba, Elodea,* or water sprite can be retained for planting in another tank or for starting new clumps of plants in the original tank. Sometimes hair-like algae spread through the tank, covering rocks and plants with long green threads. These algae can be removed from the plants by gently passing your fingers through the foliage and scooping out the floating threads with a net.

A certain amount of sediment or mulm will build up on the surface of the gravel bed. This sediment consists of dead pieces of plants, decomposed remains of uneaten food particles, and fish droppings. Some of this material

A young red and white oranda, 8 months old. Years ago headgrowth was a slow process, taking up to two years to develop. Now, with better feeding, knowledge, and environment, it is not uncommon to see good headgrowth at six months. Photo by F. Rosenzweig.

Jikins are excellent in the aquarium and outdoor environment alike. Photo by F. Rosenzweig.

This is a fantastic calico ryukin with a small pointed face and deep back. The only drawback would be the lack of a good shoulder hump. Photo by F. Rosenzweig.

will work its way into the gravel bed and provide nourishment for rooted plants. At every water change, use a device called a "gravel washer," probing gently around plant roots and perhaps more vigorously elsewhere in the gravel to both clean the gravel and remove the water for your change.

When cleaning the outside glass of the tank, never use an aerosol ammonia-based cleaner. Plain water will clean the glass if you are conscientious about it. If you need a bit more power, you can use some white vinegar and water or one of the fish-safe glass cleaners from your pet shop.

The underside of your light canopy will need to be cleaned periodically. Vinegar and water are good for removing the mineral deposits. Just be sure to rinse thoroughly.

A beautiful solid orange lionhead ranchu with a nice thick headgrowth that is wider than the body. Photo by F. Rosenzweig.

KEEPING GOLDFISH OUTDOORS

Many varieties of goldfish are at their best in outdoor ponds, and the advantages of keeping them in ponds are many. There are usually no aeration problems as the large surface area allows a substantial interchange of gases to take place, plants will grow more freely in sunlight, and there will be plenty of beneficial natural food available for the fish. Goldfish grown in ponds exhibit especially vivid colors.

SITING THE POND

No two ponds are alike. There are many methods of constructing a garden pond and it is not a project that should be rushed into without

This is a typical wood whiskey half barrel pool with a preformed liner inserted in the barrel—perfect for one or two medium-to-large goldfish.

Water gardening can be as simple as this, a preformed liner with a few plants and some goldfish.

first giving it some serious thought. Primary consideration must be given to the location of the pond. It should not be built too closely to deciduous trees, because falling leaves in autumn can cause no end of trouble. Leaves must be continually removed from the pond or they will sink, decompose, and upset the balance of a mature pond. Beyond the leaves, the roots of trees will eventually grow into the construction and cause fracturing and leakage.

The ideal site for a pond is one that receives sunlight on about half of its surface for most of the day. A totally shaded pond is no good. Aquatic plants need light, and plenty of it. Some shade is necessary for the fish in case of overheating, but in the main the pond should be sunlit.

This lovely ornament is not strictly for decoration; it helps protect the fish in the pond from predation. Herons, in particular, are solitary birds that will not typically invade another heron's territory, even if it is a replica. Photo by M. Gilroy.

The green water in this pond will contribute to high color in any goldfish kept in it. Some people protest green water, but it is often a cyclical phenomenon and as long as the nitrates aren't excessively high, it will clear in time. Photo by M. P. & C. Piednoir.

This is a formal-style pond, well suited to keeping goldfish. The fountain provides necessary water movement and aeration. Photo by M. Gilroy.

POND DESIGNS

There are many styles of ornamental pond. Some ponds are constructed of concrete and stone. Waterfalls are a big feature on others. The construction of a concrete or stone pond is a real project, the discussion of which is far beyond the scope of this book. Other types of pond, like those using pond liners or shells, are relatively easy to set up. Some people use a child's wading pool as a temporary pond. Even a giant flowerpot can be turned into a very nice "container garden." Major items like filtration, plumbing, and the creation of fountains or waterfalls are also beyond our space here, so if you are considering building a pond for your goldfish, please consult one of the many fine T.F.H. publications on ponds and water gardening before committing to a plan.

A pond should be wider than it is deep. It should be at least 18 inches deep so the water does not freeze solid in winter. Generally, ponds have a deep area and a shallow one. If the shallow area is 18 inches, the deep area can be 3 to 4 feet in depth. For the growing of pond plants, it is advisable to design the pond with an inner ledge on which to place the plants.

PLANTS IN THE POND

Goldfish ponds usually contain aquatic plants like water lilies (*Nymphaea* spp.), lotus (*Nelumbo* spp.), and a host of other plants, submerged, floating, and emerse. Marginal plants like iris, rush, and swamp lily help turn your goldfish pond into a real water garden.

"Pondering" is a family hobby. The garden pond is a classroom for young and old alike. Photo by A. Nelson.

The water-containing section of this lovely small pond was created using a 4-foot precast liner. Photo by R. Sacher.

Water lilies are a delightful feature of this small indoor goldfish pool. Needless to say, water lilies require abundant light to grow and blossom. Photo by M. Gilroy.

Parrot's feather (*Myriophyllum aquaticum*) and water lettuce (*Pistia stratiotes*) are commonly used plants in the outdoor goldfish pool. Photo by Dr. J. Thimes.

Ponds appear in many shapes and sizes. It's *your* pond; as long as the fish can live well in it, you can make it any style you like. Photo by M. P. & C. Piednoir.

Pond plants are usually planted in clean plastic containers in a soil mix of some kind with a gravel layer on top to prevent the soil from washing out of the container. Plants are cleaned and sterilized before being introduced to the pond. Dead and damaged leaves are removed.

FANCY GOLDFISH VARIETIES IN THE POND

Some fancy goldfish are more pond-worthy than others are. Some ponds are more hospitable to fancy goldfish than others. If you know your pond and you know your fish, you shouldn't have any trouble deciding whether or not to include a fish in the pond. Any concerns about placing a particular goldfish in your pond revolve around possible damage to the fish in the

Water hyacinth (*Eichhornia crassipes*) is treasured for its ability to remove nitrate from the water. It is very useful in ponds but *must not* be released into natural waterways, where it causes immense problems for wildlife management personnel. Photo by J. Tyson.

Marginal plantings are delightful additions to the pond decor. Planters provide natural barriers against people and animals accidentally falling into the pond. Photo by J. Tyson.

"uncontrolled" environment of the pond. Small, protected ponds are usually better for fancy varieties than the large, naturally occurring "duck pond" that came with the house and doubled the mortgage. Obviously, it is not good to mix speedy slim fish with "waddlers," goldfish that can barely swim for their golfball-shaped bodies. The competition for food would be brutal. Bubble-eyes are particularly unsuited to pond life. Any projection can puncture the eye bubble and the fish do not see well enough to avoid dangers. Some of the long-finned goldfish are fine for the "civilized" pond (where you can keep an eye on them), but again, do not keep them with fast fish like comets. If you are going to use fancy goldfish in your pond, be sure they always have the upper hand.

FEEDING GOLDFISH

One of the most frequent causes of premature death among goldfish is incorrect feeding. Overfeeding is one of the beginner's worst errors and is something that many people just cannot resist doing. Fish eat far less than you might expect, and if they are given more than they can immediately devour, the food will sink to the bottom of the aquarium or pond and pollute the water. Also, try giving them foods that they can easily find and swallow. Avoid using both small and excessively large food particles.

FEEDING GOLDFISH
The correct feeding of your fish is very important, and when possible they should be fed at the same time every day, preferably once in the morning and once in the evening. The food should always be placed in the same spot in the aquarium or pond, and the fish will soon learn to anticipate feeding time. They will beg for food every time they see you—goldfish are always hungry (or at least think they are)—but overfeeding is probably the leading cause of death in older goldfish. If for any reason a meal is missed, this will cause no harm to the fish, provided that this does not happen too often. Most fish can live quite happily for up to three or four weeks without being fed, and during this time they will obtain some nourishment by nibbling at the water plants and the algae growing in the pond or aquarium. It is not,

Goldfish are inordinately fond of live and frozen bloodworms. This is good food for them as long as they are getting the necessary amount of green foods as well. Photo by M. Staniszewski.

however, recommended that they be allowed to go without being fed for so long a period of time.

Feed the goldfish as much as they can finish in two minutes, twice a day. Feed a good-quality food and, if it is dry food, soak it in water for a few minutes to moisten it before feeding. Supplement their diets with peas that have been popped out of their skins and blanched leaf greens.

The food fishes prefer vary tremendously among different species. Some fishes are carnivorous, and some are herbivorous, but the vast majority are omnivorous, which means that they consume both animal and veg-

etable matter. Goldfish are omnivorous and should be fed accordingly, using both animal and vegetable matter in the diet.

Because fishes are cold-blooded creatures, their rate of metabolism decreases at low temperatures and they require less food. In fact, if the temperature is below 50° F, they should not be fed at all. Foods containing high percentages of fat should be avoided in cooler weather because they are too difficult for the fish to digest at that time.

Prepared Foods
Many excellent brands of dried foods are available that

are specially formulated for goldfish. While goldfish will eat almost anything, a goldfish food high in carbohydrates (plant food), with a moderate amount of protein (15%-30%) and low in fat will keep your goldfish active and healthy for many years. As in all animal feeding, a variety of foods is important to assure a balanced diet. If you feed prepared foods, you should feed two or three different kinds to give variety to the goldfish's diet. Pelleted or flake foods of the appropriate sizes are both used in the feeding of goldfish.

Older goldfish gulp a lot of air when feeding from the surface, which if swallowed can leave you with a floating fish. This floating condition usually will go away in a day or two but until it does, the fish is under a great deal of harmful stress.

It is important to presoak your dry food as goldfish that eat a lot of unsoaked dry food very quickly can have some digestive problems with constipation. This is caused by the dry food absorbing water in the intestine, leaving the fish with an impacted intestine. Another way around this problem is to feed small amounts at each feeding and to increase the number of feedings to assure they get enough to eat.

Live Foods

Prepared foods may be supplemented with live foods such as daphnia, brine shrimp, bloodworms, mosquito larvae, wingless fruit flies, etc. Goldfish have been known to live for years on a diet of dried fish food alone, but they cannot be compared, as far as growth, finnage, and color are concerned, with fish whose diet has been supplemented with live food.

Many household foods may also be given as a supplement to the daily diet, although such commodities should not become the sole diet, as they are often lacking certain vitamins. Bread crumbs, breakfast cereals, boiled potatoes, shredded spinach or lettuce, minced lean beef and many other table foods can be offered to the fish in small quantities. These foods make a welcome change to the normal basic diet and are usually eaten greedily by most goldfish.

The value of live foods in the diet should not be underestimated. The results of their use make it well worth the extra trouble necessary to obtain various suitable live foods.

Earthworms are one of the most valuable live foods and are especially useful during the breeding season. Whole earthworms are usually too big for small- to medium-size fish, but large pond-raised goldfish can consume them whole. For smaller fish, the worms must be chopped into smaller pieces.

Prepared foods are available in many shapes and sizes. Adjust the size of the food according to the fish. Photo by M. P. & C. Piednoir.

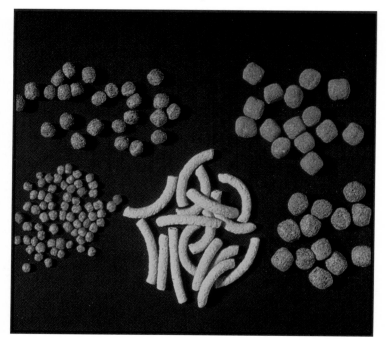

Frozen Foods

There are a great many nutritious and wholesome frozen foods available in the freezer compartment of your local pet shop. Frozen brine shrimp, bloodworms, winged insects, etc. will all be appreciated by your goldfish. There are also a number of vegetable and fish combinations that are ideal for goldfish. Be careful not to overfeed. Brine shrimp, fresh or frozen should be rinsed before introduction to the tank.

BREEDING GOLDFISH

After you've had the goldfish for a while, you might notice that some of them seem to be getting quite heavy. This might seem odd, since they are all eating about the same amount of food. It is likely that the heavier ones are females who are filling with roe (ripe eggs). This usually occurs in early spring, just prior to the beginning of the spring breeding season. A close look at the thinner goldfish may reveal tiny white pimples on the head and gill covers. These are breeding tubercles, which appear only on males and only during the breeding season. Once the breeding season is over, the tubercles disappear.

There are two methods for breeding goldfish; one is the natural method in which the fish are bred in very large aquaria or preferably in ponds, and the other method is by artificial insemination. Unless you intend to go into a large-scale breeding program, the pond method is preferred because it is simpler.

THE POND METHOD

One of the leading breeders of goldfish in the early part of the 20th century was Dr. Shinnosuke Matsubara. In 1908 he presented a paper in Washington DC entitled "Goldfish and Their Culture in Japan." In this paper he described the entire breeding and rearing process of the well-known ranchu goldfish,

This excellent specimen is the product of many generations of careful selective breeding. Photo by F. Rosenzweig.

which is still a popular variety even today. Dr. Matsubara's method is as applicable today as it was in 1908 and serves equally well for nearly any of the goldfish varieties available.

When the breeding is carried out on a small scale, the usual number of parent fish is five, two females and three males. But for large-scale breeding it is best to use a 50-50 ratio of males to females. Spawning usually occurs anywhere from the beginning of April to about the middle of May. For the best results, careful attention should be given to the fish during September, October,

and November of the preceding year. During that time plenty of live food should be given to them, but without overfeeding them. The males should be separated from the females sometime before the breeding season begins.

As the spawning season approaches, the water in the pond should not be changed, but the goldfish should be amply fed with mosquito larvae, earthworms or tubifex worms for about ten days.

At the end of the heavy feeding period, as the water temperature begins to rise or when it rains, spawning will occur. This usually happens when the water temperature has risen to about 50 to 65 F. A day or two before the anticipated start of the spawning, the water in the pond should be at least partially changed. The parent fish should be removed when the spawning is complete. The spawning bed consists of dense clusters of *Myriophyllum verticillatum* upon which the adhesive eggs are deposited usually the morning after the water change.

The pond size for five breeders should be three feet wide by four feet long and should be about five feet deep. Larger areas are required if more breeders are to be used. After the spawning is over and the breeders have been removed from the pond, the water in the pond should be drained quite low. Alternatively, the eggs can be removed by carefully lifting them out of the pond and placing them in shallow tanks containing water drained from the pond.

The eggs will hatch in eight to nine days when the water is kept at 60 to 65° F, and for a few days, while their last remaining yolk is being absorbed, the fry do not move about very much. For the most part they will stay on the gravel bottom or in the plant clusters. Three days after hatching the fry begin to swim free and feed. They can be fed at first with hardboiled egg yolk that has been strained through a piece of very fine cheesecloth. Mix the strained yolk with water until the water has a dense yellow color, then sprinkle the mixture over the entire tank. After seven days of feeding the fry with this egg yolk mixture, they will be large enough to begin to feed on sifted *Daph-*

nia or *Cyclops* or on newly hatched brine shrimp. When the goldfish fry have fed on these small creatures for about 15 days, they should be large enough to begin to feed on small mosquito larvae, finely chopped earthworms or tubifex worms.

HAND METHODS OF BREEDING GOLDFISH

The entire secret for success in this method of breeding goldfish depends upon the proper selection of ripe breeding stock.

The male must have a good supply of sperm and the female must be well loaded with ripe eggs. To test this criterion for the male, catch one in a net and press gently with one finger on his midsection just above and slightly forward of the vent. This should produce an excretion of milky fluid from his vent; this fluid contains the sperm. The female is checked in the same manner except that you look for small yellowish eggs instead of while milky exudate. Once the pair has been selected, they should be placed into a small, clean aquarium containing water from which they have been taken. The male should then be held in such a manner that his vent is below the surface of the water and the top part of his body above the water line. He should be squeezed gently, as before, but for a longer period of time as you move him about in the tank, spreading his milt throughout the water. Place him back in the pond or aquarium from which he came. The same thing should now be done to the female. If she is ripe enough, several thousand

eggs can be produced. After all her eggs are "milked," she should be placed back in her original pond or aquarium. The water in the small tank should now be stirred for a minute or two so that the eggs and sperm will have a better chance of coming into contact with one another. The tank in which this artificial insemination takes place need not exceed one gallon in capacity, but could be a little larger if your breeders are fairly large. A clean mixing bowl can even be used for this purpose, but of course one fish cannot be kept in the bowl while the other is being milked.

About eight hours later the water should be poured out of the insemination tank. The eggs will be quite sticky and will adhere to the sides of the container. Pouring the water off rids it of dead and unfertilized eggs and the unused sperm. The small tank or bowl should now be placed into a much larger aquarium or pond containing only some old conditioned water from the original breeding pond and perhaps the beginning of an infusoria culture (microscopic organisms upon which the fry will be able to feed after they are free-swimming). The water in this aquarium or pond should be just deep enough to cover the insemination container by a few inches. When the eggs hatch and the fry show signs of moving about, they should be gently poured out of the small tank and into the larger quarters. From this point on the young are handled the same way they are in the natural breeding technique.

GOLDFISH HEALTH

Although millions of common goldfish die annually at an early age under the crowded and unhealthy conditions of the goldfish bowl, goldfish are a long-lived type of fish. Under reasonable keeping conditions, they should live for ten to twenty years in the aquarium. Pond-kept goldfish—provided raccoons, herons, or the neighbor's cat does not eat them—can live for as long as thirty years.

Fancy goldfish are usually not so long-lived. There are a lot of culls in a spawn of fancy goldfish, especially as the features become more bizarre. Many of the young do not live beyond a few weeks. Of the survivors, a goodly number will die in the first year. Beyond that, with good care and barring unfortunate accidents, pet fancy goldfish can have a normal lifespan of a decade or more.

Goldfish are hardy and adaptable creatures. When they succumb to parasites, fungi, or virus infections, it is usually because a poor environment has weakened them.

Symptoms to watch for in ailing goldfish are: loss of appetite; sluggish and aimless swimming; folded or clamped fins; hanging from the surface or lying on the bottom; slow reactions to disturbances; rubbing against surfaces as if trying to scrape something off its body; loss of luster; ragged fins, lesions, spots or bumps; bloating or

The deformed gill on this goldfish makes it a poor candidate. Be sure to examine any fish you plan to purchase carefully.

emaciation; and gills that are pale rather than flushed with a healthy red color.

Exotic goldfish are more vulnerable to disease than the simpler varieties are and require more care. Fry are exceedingly delicate and are nearly impossible to successfully treat for diseases. If your goldfish exhibit any of these symptoms, consider carefully what might have caused the trouble.

Have there been any new fish or plants introduced into the aquarium or has water of doubtful purity been added, possibly introducing parasites or diseases? Is there adequate

aeration? Are the fish overcrowded or has their environment generally deteriorated? Have the fish been handled roughly or has the water been changed without the proper precautions of temperature adjustments or chlorine removal? Have the fish been fed inferior or improper foods or has the water been polluted by adding more food than the fish can eat? These questions should be considered carefully, as their answers might provide a clue as to what is wrong with your goldfish. Often, simply correcting the problems in the environment can eliminate troubles, but sometimes chemical treatment is necessary.

Medications can be administered either by direct application to the affected area or by dissolving them in the water, depending upon what the medication is and what you are trying to cure. If the substance is to be dissolved, be sure that there are no undissolved particles remaining or the fish may eat these, with disastrous results. To make sure there are no undissolved particles of medication being introduced into the tank, filter the solution through a clean piece of linen or a brine shrimp net before adding it to the water.

Many patented drugs are available for treating specific diseases, and the average aquarist is usually well advised to stay with these. Be wary of any substance that is claimed to be a cure for everything.

If individual goldfish are showing any disease symptoms, they should be isolated immediately. If the entire pond or aquarium is affected, then large-scale measures must be taken. If the exact trouble is not known, general first aid measures must be taken. A water temperature of at least 60° F must be maintained, adequate aeration must be provided and only live food should be fed. The water level should be lowered to 4 to 6 inches so that distressed fish do not have to struggle to reach food and the well oxygenated surface water.

THE HOSPITAL TANK

If individuals require treatment, they should be isolated from the rest of the goldfish to prevent possible spread of the malady. A small hospital tank should be maintained for this purpose. It should contain no gravel or plants. It should have a stable temperature and should be situated in a quiet place, away from bright lights, where the fish will not be excited or disturbed. When the fish is transferred to the hospital tank, as much of its original water as possible should be included to minimize the shock of transfer.

The use of an isolation tank prevents a sick fish from infecting healthy fish. Medications can be used freely in it without worrying about killing plants and other beneficial organisms that normally inhabit tanks and ponds. More accurate dosages can be administered because of the smaller volume of water in the isolation tank. Healthy fish will not be able to harass weakened individuals, and once treatment is completed the tank can be easily sterilized.

An ailing fish can be noticed quickly in an aquarium, but in a pond, where there are many fish and many places for them to hide, it is not so easy to detect the symptoms of a disease until quite a few fish have been affected. The pond keeper must always be on the alert. If any fish appears to be slightly off color or behaves abnormally in any way, it should be netted out and placed in an isolation aquarium.

Disinfecting the Fish

A strong salt bath is the most effective method of disinfecting goldfish, particularly when they have open sores that leave them vulnerable to infection.

One pound of non-iodized salt should be dissolved in three gallons of water. For this, it is best to use some of the water the fish are already in. The netted fish should be dipped into this solution for a minute or so, then immediately transferred to freshly aged water in the hospital tank. The fish may be stunned for a short time but will soon recover. Some of the mucous coating may be shed, but this won't harm the fish if it is isolated for awhile.

Injuries

Injuries are usually due to rough handling, but vigorous spawning activities, other fish, birds, or insects can also cause them. Injuries that do not cause the immediate death of the fish will usually heal without treatment, but the goldfish should still be protected against infection. The injured fish can be netted and the wounds dabbed with tincture of iodine. A light coating of petroleum jelly can then be smeared over the wounds and the fish should be placed in isolation until it has recovered.

Surface Hanging

Surface hanging can be a symptom of overcrowding, pollution, or gill flukes. The pollution could be caused by decomposing organic matter or a high concentration of metal, particularly copper, dissolved in the water while passing through the water pipes. Never place copper or brass objects in an aquarium, and before using fresh water, it should be run for a minute or so to allow water that was in the copper pipes to run out.

Gas Bubble Disease

This problem is caused by excessive oxygen or other gases dissolved in the water, usually due to brisk aeration and rampant plant growth together with strong sunlight. The problem is more prevalent in the winter since cold water retains more gases than warm water does. Air bubbles will be seen adhering to the bodies and fins of the goldfish, and they will often float at the surface on their sides. The fish are experiencing excessive gases in their blood stream. This condition is similar to the bends experienced by deep-sea divers. Long-finned goldfish seem more prone to suffer from gas bubble disease than short-finned goldfish. This problem can be easily remedied by placing the fish into fresh water that is free of any algae or by gently agitating the water to release the gases.

White Spot (*Ichthyophthirius multifiliis*)

These small spherical parasites appear commonly on tropical fishes, and they can attack goldfish, too. The minute white spots initially scattered over the body and later covering the head and gills easily identify this affliction. Once the gills have become affected, respiration will be impaired and the fish may soon suffocate. Fish frequently rub themselves in an attempt to ease the irritation.

The reddish lesions on this fish are caused by a fungal condition and can be cured if caught in time. If neglected, the fish will die in a matter of days.

There are patented medicines made largely of malachite green that are available for this condition, but an experienced aquarist may be able to treat an affected fish by placing it in a hospital tank and gradually increasing the temperature to just over 85 F.

In a pond where the problem is persistent, disinfection may be necessary. The fish should be removed from the pond and chlorinated lime should be introduced into the water. After a day or two, adding the same quantity of sodium thiosulfate to the water can neutralize the disinfectant. The pond should then be drained, rinsed, and refilled.

Anchor Worm

Anchor worms are small free-swimming parasites that get their name from the shape of the head. They burrow into the flesh of the fish, leaving only the egg sac protruding. It is the egg sac that reveals the presence of the parasite. It is often up to one-half inch in length and can be easily seen. These parasites are often seen behind the dorsal and pectoral fins. Soon after one attaches itself, a red blood spot will be seen at the point of entry. When the fish is lifted out of the water, the worm contracts into a small fleshy blob.

Using a cotton swab, the individual parasites should be painted with either turpentine

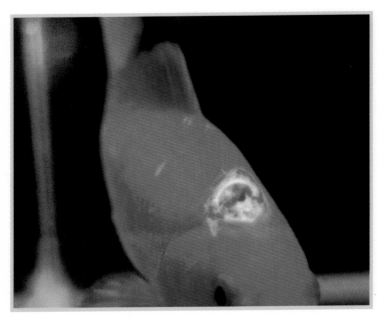

This comet goldfish is suffering from an open wound. It could be an ulcer from a bacterial infection or a simple laceration. In any case, it needs treatment. Photo by Dr. E. Johnson.

or kerosene. This softens the parasite and enables it to be easily removed with tweezers, thus causing the minimum amount of damage to the fish. If an attempt is made to remove the parasites without first killing them, pieces of fish flesh will be pulled out with the parasites. Particular care must always be taken when removing them near the eyes or gill membranes. Once they have been removed, the affected areas should be painted with an antiseptic such as Merbromin to guard against bacterial infection.

Fish Louse

This free-swimming parasite is very difficult to detect because it is fairly translucent and fastens itself tightly against the body of the fish. It is flat, round, approximately one-eighth of an inch in diameter and

possesses a small proboscis between its eyes, which is used to extract blood from its host. It is often found on the belly, gills, and throat of a fish. It can live up to three days without a host, and it lays rows of eggs on the aquarium glass.

A good indication that fish lice are present in the tank or pond is when the goldfish rub themselves against objects in an attempt to scrape the parasites from their bodies. Often they cause more damage to themselves in this manner than the fish lice cause. In a severe attack, the fish can become so weak that they die. Affected areas become inflamed and flushed in color.

For the aquarist working on a small scale, it is usually simplest to remove the parasites individually by painting them with either turpentine or kerosene and

then removing the dead parasites with tweezers.

If a severe attack has become established, it is best to make a solution of one gram of potassium permanganate to 22 gallons of water. Immerse the fish for approximately 20 minutes every ten days until all of the parasites have been exterminated. This repetition is necessary because the parasites in the egg stage are not affected.

Flukes

These parasites are barely visible to the naked eye, and they can only be suspected until the infestation is severe. Affected fish swim in an erratic and jerky manner and usually appear to be exhausted. The fish may twitch and attempt to scrape the flukes off by rubbing their bodies against objects. The growth of the fish will be retarded and, in severe cases, the flukes may be visible underneath the gill covers. Blood may also be visible on the skin.

Flukes are free-swimming parasites that flourish best in an overcrowded tank. They are usually lethal to fry. If flukes are suspected in any fish, all of the fish in the same environment must be treated for the parasite.

A patented formula of formalin and malachite green is recommended for the treatment of flukes. Since concentrations differ by manufacturer, follow the directions on the bottle carefully. Repeat the treatment at weekly intervals for three weeks, being sure to perform a large water change both before and at the end of each treatment.